THE REVOLT OF
THE REVOLT OF
THE ENGLISH MAJORS
THE ENGLISH MAJORS

Recent Doonesbury Books by G.B. Trudeau

Special Collections

A DOONESBURY BOOK

THE REVOLT OF
THE REVOLT OF
THE ENGLISH MAJORS
THE ENGLISH MAJORS

BY G. B. TRUDEAU

Andrews McMeel
Publishing

Kansas City

DOONESBURY is distributed internationally by Universal Press Syndicate.

The Revolt of the English Majors copyright © 2001 by G. B. Trudeau. All rights reserved. Printed in the United States of America. No part of this book may be used or reproduced in any manner whatsoever without written permission except in the case of reprints in the context of reviews. For information, write Andrews McMeel Publishing, an Andrews McMeel Universal company, 4520 Main Street, Kansas City, Missouri 64111.

03 04 05 BAM 10 9 8 7 6 5 4 3 2

ISBN: 0-7407-1847-9

Library of Congress Catalog Card Number: 2001090186

DOONESBURY may be viewed on the Internet at:
www.uexpress.com and www.doonesbury.com

——— **ATTENTION: SCHOOLS AND BUSINESSES** ———

Andrews McMeel books are available at quantity discounts with bulk purchase for educational, business, or sales promotional use. For information, please write to: Special Sales Department, Andrews McMeel Publishing, 4520 Main Street, Kansas City, Missouri 64111.

"If you're asking me as the president, would I understand reality, I do."

—George W. Bush

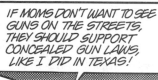

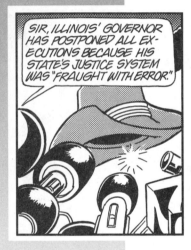

9

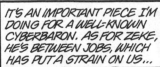

HI, J.J., IT'S...

HI, THIS IS J.J.! SORRY I CAN'T COME TO THE PHONE. I'M WORKING ON A COMMISSION.

IT'S AN IMPORTANT PIECE I'M DOING FOR A WELL-KNOWN CYBERBARON. AS FOR ZEKE, HE'S BETWEEN JOBS, WHICH HAS PUT A STRAIN ON US...

FORTUNATELY, THE SEX IS STILL OFF THE CHARTS. LEAVE A MESSAGE. ≈BEEP!≈

GACK!

GACK?

MUST BE MIKE.

ANYWAY, IT'D INVOLVE OUR MOVING BACK TO CONNECTICUT...

FORGET IT! NO **WAY** YOU'RE TAKING ALEX TO ANOTHER STATE!

WELL, WHAT AM I SUPPOSED TO DO, J.J.? I NEED TO EARN A LIVING!

TELECOMMUTE. OR BUY THE COMPANY. KIDS ALWAYS GO FOR CASH.

HMM... YOU KNOW, THAT'S NOT SUCH A CRAZY IDEA. WITHOUT THEM, THE CONCEPT'S A GOLD MINE.

WHICH'D PUT MY DREAM WITHIN REACH, TOO.

YOUR DREAM?

TO SUE YOU. YOU'RE USUALLY BROKE.

THAT WAS BIG PAUL. HE SAYS WE GOTTA MOVE OUT TO MAKE ROOM FOR THE SUMMER SCHOOL KIDS!

JUST AS WELL, DUDE...

WE'VE ALREADY OUTGROWN ROSENBLATT HALL. IF WE'RE GOING TO GROW A BILLION-DOLLAR BUSINESS BY CHRISTMAS, WE NEED TO FIND SOME **SERIOUS** SQUARE FOOTAGE!

WITH HUNDREDS OF FULFILLMENT EMPLOYEES, WE'LL BE NEEDING AT LEAST... YO, JUST GOT AN E-MAIL FROM OUR FUTURE CEO...

HE WANTS TO BUY US OUT FOR $5,000.

TAKE IT! **TAKE IT!**

AL, I'VE BEEN GIVING A LOT OF THOUGHT TO WHY YOU'RE NOT DOING BETTER IN THE POLLS...

AND I THINK THE ANSWER IS OBVIOUS: PEOPLE WILL ALWAYS PREFER THE CLASS CLOWN TO THE CLASS NERD...

THE FACT IS, AL, THE AMERICAN PEOPLE DON'T REALLY WANT SOMEONE **TOO** SMART FOR PRESIDENT.

BUT... BUT **YOU'RE** EVEN SMARTER THAN **I** AM!

YEAH, BUT EVER NOTICE HOW I DO REALLY DUMB THINGS? THERE'S A REASON.

AL, YOU HAVE TO LEARN TO STOP MAKING CONNECTIONS BETWEEN THINGS. YOU HAVE TO SIMPLIFY YOUR MESSAGE...

EVER LISTEN TO BUSH ON FOREIGN POLICY? "IT'S A DIFFERENT WORLD. THE WORLD HAS CHANGED." HE SAYS IT OVER AND OVER AGAIN.

NEVER MIND THAT THE COLD WAR ACTUALLY ENDED TEN YEARS AGO. YOU NEED AN INSIGHT THAT BANAL.

HOW ABOUT "IT'S A SMALL WORLD"?

TOO QUANTITATIVE, IT CAN'T SOUND JUDGMENTAL.

YOU KNOW, AL, YOU MIGHT ALSO WANT TO REACTIVATE YOUR DOWN-HOME ACCENT...

IT CERTAINLY WORKS FOR BUSH. EVERY TIME HE OPENS HIS MOUTH, THE IVY LEAGUE PEDIGREE EVAPORATES...

HE PRONOUNCES NUCLEAR AS "NUKULAR," AND HE CAN'T SAY SOCIAL SECURITY WITHOUT SPRAYING EVERYONE WITHIN FIVE FEET.

SO I NEED A SPEECH IMPEDIMENT?

RIGHT. OR ARRIVE DRUNK. ANYTHING TO SOFTEN YOU.

HERE'S SOMETHING ELSE YOU COULD LEARN FROM DUBYA, AL...

SINCE BEING SEEN AS A KNOW-IT-ALL OBVIOUSLY HAS A DOWNSIDE, LET OTHER PEOPLE CARRY THE LOAD FOR YOU.

DID YOU SEE BUSH'S RECENT FOREIGN POLICY ADDRESS? HE SURROUNDED HIMSELF WITH PEOPLE LIKE HENRY KISSINGER, GEORGE SHULTZ AND BRENT SCOWCROFT. NOW *THAT'S* THROW-WEIGHT!

BUT... BUT IT LOOKED LIKE MADAME TUSSAUD'S UP THERE!

WELL, YEAH, MAKE SURE YOUR GUYS BLINK.

AL, YOU HAVE TO CO-OPT WHAT'S WORKING FOR THE OTHER GUY. FOR INSTANCE, BUSH SAYS OVER AND OVER THAT THE BEST DECISION HE EVER MADE WAS TO MARRY HIS WIFE...

...BUT THAT HE'S NOT SURE MARRYING HIM WAS THE BEST DECISION *SHE* EVER MADE. IMPLICATION: AS IF! CLOYING AND INSINCERE AS THE LINE MAY BE, IT WORKS.

HOLD ON — I SHOULD SAY TIPPER COULD HAVE DONE BETTER?

SOMETHING LIKE THAT.

BUT I WAS A *PRIME* CATCH!

LOOK, YOU WANT THE LAUGH OR NOT?

YOU KNOW, AL, THIS ELECTION SURE HAS A FAMILIAR FEEL TO IT...

TWO CANDIDATES WITH ELITE CREDENTIALS, BUT ONLY ONE OF THEM IN TOUCH WITH THOSE HE WOULD LEAD...

IT'S LIKE THE '92 ELECTION ALL OVER AGAIN!

EXCEPT THAT I PLAY BUSH.

RIGHT. WHOM I CREAMED.

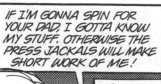

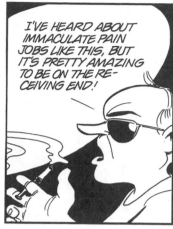

UNCLE DUKE, WE NEED TO TALK ABOUT HOW WE WANT ALL THIS TO PLAY IN THE MEDIA...

AS YOUR COMMUNICATIONS MAN, I'D BE DERELICT IF I DIDN'T ADVISE YOU TO TAKE FULLEST ADVANTAGE OF THIS UNFORTUNATE INCIDENT!

HMM...YES, I SEE WHAT YOU MEAN...

GOOD MORNING!

MORNING? ARE YOU SURE?

...AND MULTIPLE CONTUSIONS TOO NUMEROUS TO ENUMERATE...

ALL THANKS TO ONE PATRICK J. BUCHANAN!

WHERE DOES HE THINK HE IS? THIS ISN'T WEIMAR GERMANY! IT ISN'T AUSTRIA! IT ISN'T CANADA! THIS IS **AMERICA**!

ANYWAY, THE DOCTORS ARE HOPEFUL.

IT'S JUST **SOUTH** OF CANADA! YOU CAN'T MISS IT!

ALSO, THERE MAY BE A LITTLE BRAIN DAMAGE, BUT IT'S NOTHING I CAN'T HANDLE!

MR. DUKE, WILL YOU BE SUING MR. BUCHANAN?

NO! I WILL **NOT** BE DISTRACTED FROM MY GOAL, WHICH FROM THE START HAS BEEN...

UM...

MATCHING FUNDS, NO?

YEAH, HOW MUCH DO YOU THINK I COULD GET?

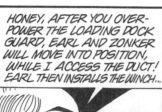

WELL, IT'S ALL UP TO ORATOR AL NOW. HE BETTER HOPE HE CAN RECONCILE ALL THOSE VERSIONS OF HIMSELF...

TONIGHT MAY BE HIS LAST CHANCE TO CREATE A COHERENT RATIONALE FOR HIS CANDIDACY...

HOLD ON TO THOSE BON MOTS, RICK! I'D LIKE TO USE YOU IN A WEBCAST, OKAY?

UM... OKAY.

THIS IS ROLAND HEDLEY® TALKING LIVE TO RICK REDFERN OF THE WASHINGTON POST! FOR AOL-TIME-WARNER-YAP!.COM, I'M ROLAND HEDLEY®!

BUT... BUT I DIDN'T SAY ANYTHING!

WE WERE RUNNING LONG. YOU SHOULD'VE JUMPED IN.

FROM LOS ANGELES, WITH ANOTHER POLITICAL CONVENTION UNDER HIS BELT, THIS IS ROLAND HEDLEY®!

SO WHAT'D YOU THINK OF GORE'S SPEECH, ROLAND?

HIS SPEECH?

UM... I THOUGHT IT WAS ABOUT WHAT WE COULD'VE EXPECTED. WHETHER HE DID WHAT HE HAD TO DO REMAINS TO BE SEEN!

YOU WATCHED THE "E.R." RERUN, DIDN'T YOU?

UM... YEAH. DIDN'T EVERYONE?

WELL, SEE YOU ON THE TRAIL, ROLAND...

GOOD LORD!

WHAT?

THE YAP!.COM TRAFFIC REPORT— OUR NUMBERS TREND IS INCREDIBLE!

WE HAD ONLY 2,435 DAILY VISITORS FOR THE G.O.P. CONVENTION, BUT FOR THE DEMOCRATS, WE HAD 4,770!

SO THE DEMAND FOR TINY, JERKY VIDEOS THAT NEVER PLAY HAS NEARLY DOUBLED!

RIGHT! NOW, **THAT'S** BRAND BUILDING!

JIM ANDREWS, LONG-TIME CEO OF UNIVERSAL PETROLEUM, IS LOST IN SWEET REVERIE.

HE DREAMS OF A PLACE WHERE A MAN CAN CONTROL HIS OWN DESTINY, SET HIS OWN LIMITS, EVEN WRITE THE LAWS THAT REGULATE HIS OWN BEHAVIOR...

A PLACE SO FRIENDLY TO THE ENTREPRENEURIAL SPIRIT THAT IT ENJOYS THE HIGHEST LEVELS OF TOXIC RELEASES AND AIR AND WATER POLLUTION IN THE COUNTRY!

YES, HE DREAMS OF TEXAS.

FOR JIM ANDREWS, TOP DOG AT UNIVERSAL PETROLEUM, IT IS A NIGHT OF LONGING.

ALTHOUGH HIS NEWEST TROPHY WIFE BREATHES SOFTLY IN THE DARKNESS BESIDE HIM, HE YEARNS ONLY FOR TEXAS, FOR THE SWEET REGULATORY RELIEF ONLY **SHE** CAN PROVIDE HIM.

TEXAS— WHERE POLLUTERS WRITE THE ENVIRONMENTAL LAWS, AND COMPLIANCE IS **VOLUNTARY!** HOW **GRAND** IT'D BE TO LIVE IN SUCH A PLACE! AND THEN IT HITS HIM ...

HE **DOES** LIVE IN SUCH A PLACE.

I'M TEXAN!

PINCH ME!

WHERE, SWEET BUNS?

IT'S 3:00 A.M. IN GEORGE DUBYA BUSH'S TEXAS.

CHERYLEE, I JUST HAD THE BEST DREAM!

THAT'S NICE, JIMMY.

I DREAMT I WAS IN TEXAS, AND GOVERNMENT WAS DOING WHAT GOVERNMENT IS SUPPOSED TO DO—WHICH IS GET OUT OF THE WAY OF BUSINESS. BUT THE DREAM IS **REAL**.

IT'S ABOUT FREEDOM, CHERYLEE! IN DUBYA'S TEXAS, I'M FREE TO RUN MY REFINERIES AS I SEE FIT, JUST AS YOU'RE FREE TO FILL YOUR DAYS WITH... UH...

WHATEVER IT IS YOU FILL YOUR DAYS WITH!

SHOPPING AND SURGERY. YOU'RE SWEET TO WONDER.

IF THE GOING WAS ROUGH ON THE HUSTINGS RECENTLY...

THIS CAMPAIGN NOT ONLY HEARS THE VOICES OF THE ENTREPRENEURS AND THE FARMERS AND THE ENTREPRENEURS! *

*ALL DIALOGUE VERBATIM 8/22/00

WHEN WE CARRY IOWA IN NOVEMBER, IT'LL MEAN THE END OF FOUR YEARS OF CLINTON-GORE!

IT'S GOING TO BE THE FINAL NAIL ON THE COFFIN.

WE CANNOT LET TERRORISTS AND ROGUE NATIONS HOLD THIS NATION HOSTILE!

I WILL WORK TO END TERRORS AND TARIFFS!

THINGS WERE EVEN WORSE IN THE SPIN PIT.

UM... WE THINK HE NEEDS MORE NAPS.

A BAD DAY FOR "THE ENGLISH PATIENT"...

OUR BUDGET'S GOING TO GROW FROM ROUGHLY $1.9 BILLION...

*VERBATIM, 8/22/00

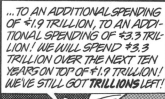

...TO AN ADDITIONAL SPENDING OF $1.9 TRILLION, TO AN ADDITIONAL SPENDING OF $3.3 TRILLION! WE WILL SPEND $3.3 TRILLION OVER THE NEXT TEN YEARS ON TOP OF $1.9 TRILLION! WE'VE STILL GOT TRILLIONS LEFT!

WHEW!

...AND A WORSE ONE FOR THE ENGLISH MAJORS.

WHAT THE HELL?...

HOW MANY ZEROS DO YOU CARRY?

1.9! NO, 3.3!

THE REVOLT OF THE ENGLISH MAJORS.

DUBYA'S TAX NUMBERS MAKE NO SENSE!

HE'S USING BILLIONS AND TRILLIONS INTERCHANGEABLY!

LOOK, GUYS, THE GOVERNOR WAS TIRED. HE FORGOT HIS FEATHER PILLOW ON THE PLANE, AND HE DIDN'T GET A NAP. SO CUT HIM SOME SLACK, OKAY?

BESIDES, FROM NOW ON HE'LL BE USING ACTUAL FAMILIES TO EXPLAIN THE PLAN. EVEN YOU PEOPLE SHOULD BE ABLE TO UNDERSTAND IT!

AND KARL WOULD GET $1200, CINDY $2500, AND JUNIOR $1.9 BILLION!

YES!

YOU KNOW, IT'S NOT LIKE LIEBERMAN IS THE ONLY POLITICIAN WITH FAITH, REV...

NO, BUT MOST OTHERS JUST USE IT TO POLISH THEIR HALOS.

WITH THIS GUY, THERE'S A SENSE THAT HIS FAITH ANIMATES HIS COMMITMENT TO A GREATER GOOD. AND THIS RESONATES WITH THE PASTORAL COMMUNITY.

THE MESSAGE OF THE RELIGIOUS RIGHT HAS ALWAYS BEEN, "OUR WAY OR THE HIGHWAY TO HELL." BUT AN INCLUSIVE GOD CARRIES A MUCH DIFFERENT MESSAGE...

"HOLD ON TO YOUR WALLET"?

NO, NO, HE'S MORE RESPONSIBLE NOW.

LOOK, SCOT, LET'S CALL THIS THING WHAT IT REALLY IS, OKAY?

WHEN YOU TALK ABOUT RESTORING A "JUST, INCLUSIVE" GOD TO PUBLIC LIFE, YOU'RE TALKING IN CODE!

WHAT YOU'RE REALLY TALKING ABOUT IS RESTORING AN ACTIVIST GOD, A LIBERAL GOD— A MARXIST GOD!

MARXISTS, INCONVENIENTLY, ARE GODLESS.

EXACTLY! SO WHO'S FOOLING WHO?

YOU KNOW, REV, LIEBERMAN MAY TALK ABOUT AN INCLUSIVE GOD WHO LOVES JUSTICE...

BUT HE HIMSELF IS NOT SO INCLUSIVE WHEN IT COMES TO WHAT REALLY MATTERS TO PEOPLE — POPULAR CULTURE!

IN JOE LIEBERMAN'S PERFECT WORLD, I WOULDN'T BE ABLE TO WATCH THE LATEST BRUTAL, MISOGYNIST CRAP FROM HOLLYWOOD!

WHICH A JUST GOD WOULD WANT FOR YOU, YOU FEEL.

RIGHT. HE WOULDN'T SEE THE HARM IN IT.

THE BEE WOULD BE NO-HOLDS-BARRED! WE'D BE PRONOUNCING BIG-TIME WORDS LIKE "SOCIAL SECURITY" AND "NUCLEAR"!

THE CONTEST WOULD THEN BE VOTED ON BY THE JURY OF SCANTILY CLAD COMMUN-ICATIONS MAJORS. OKAY, I'LL TAKE QUESTIONS NOW.

MR. DUKE, WHY ISN'T VICE PRES-IDENT GORE INVOLVED?

UM... WE CONSIDERED AL, BUT IT DIDN'T WORK OUT.

SOUNDS GREAT! WOULD WE BE RECITING THE LATIN ROOTS?

NEVER MIND.

HE'S CLAIMING HABEAS CORPUS CHRISTI? NO WAY! LET HIM GET A WHIFF OF TEXAS-STYLE JUS-TICE! THAT IT?

JUST ONE MORE MATTER, SIR...

THERE'S A FRINGE CANDIDATE NAMED DUKE WHO'S CHAL-LENGED YOU TO A PRONUNCIATION BEE.

A PRONUN-CIATION BEE?

YES, SIR.

HE'S TRYING TO MAKE ME LOOK RIDICULISTIC, ISN'T HE?

WE THINK SO.

GOVERNOR, WILL YOU BE ACCEPTING AMBASSADOR DUKE'S CHALLENGE TO A PRONUNCIA-TION BEE?

OF COURSE NOT! THIS IS A SERIOUS CAMPAIGN ABOUT WHAT'S IN MY HEART, NOT ON MY LIPS!

IT'S AN OBVIOUS ATTEMPT TO EMBARRASS ME! NO WAY I'M PARTICIPATING IN A PRONIT... PROCA... PRO...

...THAT GOTCHA THING.

THANK YOU, SIR.

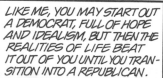

SO WHY ELSE DON'T YOU LIKE GORE, POPPY?

WELL, BECAUSE I THINK HE'LL SAY ANYTHING TO GET ELECTED.

LAST WINTER HE OPPOSED USING OUR STRATEGIC OIL SUPPLIES—NOW HE'S FOR IT. THEN HE ATTACKS HOLLYWOOD, BUT BACKS OFF AT FUND-RAISERS...

SO I GUESS I JUST DON'T FIND HIM TRUSTWORTHY.

BUT ISN'T HE SUPPOSED TO BE HANDSOME?

WELL, AGAIN, THAT'S NEW. THEY'RE JUST LIGHTING HIM BETTER.

SEE, ALEX, WHAT PUTS PEOPLE OFF ABOUT GORE IS THAT HE SEEMS ENTIRELY DRIVEN BY POLITICAL CONCERNS.

EVEN HIS BIG KISS WITH HIS WIFE AT THE CONVENTION SEEMED COMPLETELY CALCULATED.

I DUNNO, I LIKED IT. SEEING A KISS MAKES PEOPLE FEEL REASSURED AND SAFE, LIKE WHEN I SEE YOU KISS... KISS...

MY CURRENT WIFE?

OKAY, BAD EXAMPLE.

SO YOU'RE REALLY VOTING FOR BUSH? HE SEEMS KIND OF DUMB.

WELL, THAT'S ACTUALLY PART OF HIS APPEAL...

PEOPLE ARE TIRED OF BEING LED BY OUR "BEST AND BRIGHTEST," WHO TEND TO BE ARROGANT AND PATRONIZING. VOTERS ARE READY FOR ONE OF THEIR OWN!

BESIDES, HE KNOWS ENOUGH TO HIRE LOTS OF SMART PEOPLE. WHEN IT'S TIME TO GO EYEBALL-TO-EYEBALL WITH THE NEXT SADDAM HUSSEIN, HE'LL BE READY!

ARE YOU SURE? LETTERMAN CLEANED HIS CLOCK.

MONTHS AGO! HE'S MORE SEASONED NOW.

ANOTHER DAY, ANOTHER BUSH "TAX FAMILY."

WE'RE NOT TALKING FUZZY-WUZZY MATH HERE, FOLKS...

WE'RE TALKING **REAL** MONEY FOR REAL PEOPLE! FOR THE MARK SKIPPLE FAMILY, IT COULD MEAN **BILLIONS**!

Latest Slogan Latest Slogan Latest Slogan Latest Slogan Latest Slogan Latest Slogan Latest Slogan

WELL, NOT FOR THEM PERSONABLY! BUT, LOOK, THE MAN, GORE, HAS OUTSPENT ME! EVEN THOUGH MY PLAN GIVES MORE SENIORS DRUG COVERAGE! EVEN THOUGH THE INTERNET USES 8% OF OUR ENERGY!

LATER.

THOSE DON'T COUNT AS LIES, DO THEY?

NO, NO, THAT'S GORE. YOU'RE THE DUMB ONE.

W Real Sl for Real Voters

LISTEN, PEOPLE, I NEED SIMPLER NUMBERS! I STILL CAN'T EXPLAIN MY OWN TAX PROGRAM!

NOT TO WORRY, SIR, NOBODY CARES IF YOU EXAGGERATE.

WHAT DO YOU MEAN?

WELL, SIR, YOU GET STUFF WRONG ALL THE TIME, BUT SINCE IT'S OUT OF IGNORANCE, YOUR ERRORS ARE CONSIDERED "HONEST" MISTAKES.

HONEST MISTAKES?

YES, SIR.

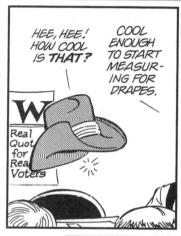

HEE, HEE! HOW COOL IS **THAT?**

COOL ENOUGH TO START MEASURING FOR DRAPES.

W Real Quot for Real Voters

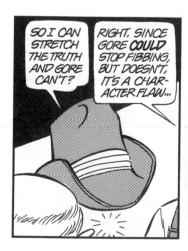

SO I CAN STRETCH THE TRUTH AND GORE CAN'T?

RIGHT, SINCE GORE **COULD** STOP FIBBING, BUT DOESN'T, IT'S A CHARACTER FLAW...

BUT BEING "THE DUMB ONE" MEANS WHEN YOU TELL A WHOPPER, YOU DON'T KNOW ANY BETTER. SO PEOPLE SEE IT AS ENDEARING, LIKE THEY DID WITH REAGAN!

WHOA...

THOSE ARE TALL BOOTS TO UNDERSTAND! I UNDERSTAND THOSE BOOTS!

I'LL ADD IT TO THE LIST...

W.

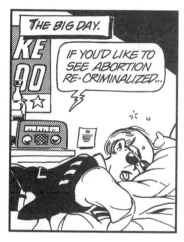

"6,000 PAIR USED SURGICAL GLOVES, 100 GROSS SWIZZLE STICKS, 3000 METRIC TONS OF COBALT..."

THEY WERE ALL GOOD DEALS, DAD.

WELL, MAYBE, BUT IT'S ALL SO RANDOM. WE HAVE TO SELL THIS STUFF. WE'LL NEVER DEVELOP A STRONG BRAND IDENTITY IF YOU JUST FREE-LANCE YOUR BUYS!

FROM NOW ON, I WANT YOU TO CLEAR EVERY PURCHASE WITH ME...

OKAY, DAD, I PROMISE. SEE YOU LATER.

UH... WHERE ARE YOU GOING?

DOWN TO THE WAREHOUSE TO FEED THE SHEEP.

I MUST HAVE BEEN CRAZY TO LET ALEX BUY FOR THE SITE. WE NOW LOOK LIKE THE WORLD'S BIGGEST E-JUNKYARD!

YEAH, WELL, THAT MAY BE, BUT I JUST CRUNCHED THE NUMBERS, AND AFTER ONLY THREE MONTHS, WE'RE ALREADY MAKING MONEY.

SWEETHEART? YOU CAN ORDER THE DEFECTIVE POODLE SKIRTS!

THANKS, DADDY.

IN THE BLACK! IN THE BLACK! WHAT A WONDERFUL PHRASE!

IT'S LIKE MUSIC, LIKE I'M HEARING IT FOR THE FIRST TIME, WHICH OF COURSE, I AM!

AND ALL BECAUSE MY TEENAGE DAUGHTER HAS A KNACK FOR PICKING OVERSTOCK!

A MILLION DUKE 2000 BUTTONS? WE'LL **TAKE** 'EM!

OKAY, HERE'S THE DILEMMA AS I SEE IT— BUSH WON TECHNICALLY, BUT GORE WON LITERALLY.

certification electors

IT'S LIKE A GAME WITH BAD OFFICIATING, WITH THE OUTCOME HINGING ON A DISPUTED CALL...

BUSH WINS IF THE REF'S WORD IS FINAL, BUT WHAT IF AN INSTANT REPLAY SHOWS GORE WON? WHICH STANDARD DO WE USE?

ANY THOUGHTS?

UM...EXCUSE ME, DUDE, DIDN'T THE DEAN BAN SPORTS ANALOGIES?

NO, ONLY IN THE BIG LECTURE COURSES.

QUESTION, MAN— IT'S INDISPUTABLE THAT MORE PEOPLE IN FLORIDA **INTEND-ED** TO VOTE FOR GORE THAN FOR BUSH...

IF GORE WINS, THE NUMBERS WILL SPEAK FOR THEMSELVES, BUT IF BUSH WINS, WON'T THE LEGITIMACY OF HIS PRESIDENCY BE FOREVER IN DOUBT?

WELL, PEOPLE HAVE SHORT MEMORIES, BUT, YEAH, THERE COULD BE A LITTLE STINK ON IT.

"PRESIDENT" BUSH!

"PRESIDENT" BUSH!

MR. "PRESI-DENT"!

SIGH...

*

...AND YOU'LL BE RESPONSI-BLE FOR CHADS, FLAGS, DIMPLES AND BUTTER-FLIES! THE QUIZ IS FRIDAY!

chad a dim

OH, YEAH? WHO SAYS? AND HOW COME **YOU** GET TO TEACH BIG PAUL'S COURSE ANY-WAY, MAN?

THE CLASS CHOSE ME YESTERDAY.

YESTERDAY? I WASN'T EVEN HERE!

ME, NEITHER!

WELL, THAT'S NOT MY FAULT, IS IT?

RE-COUNT! RE-COUNT!

OKAY, GOOD! TEACHABLE MOMENT!

82

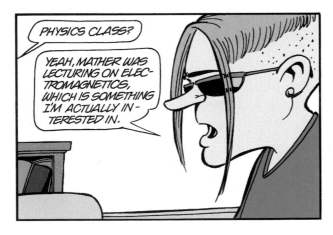

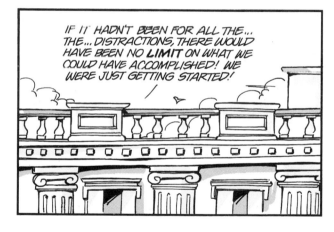

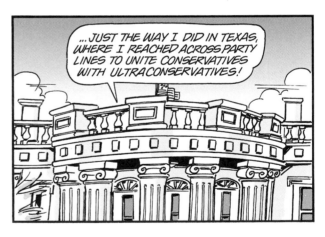

98

THE TRAIL GROWS WARMER.

YEAH, HE WAS HERE. HE SAID HE WAS GOING OVER TO THE ROYALE TAPROOM TO MEET HIS BOOKIE!

LEFT TWO HOURS AGO. HE PICKED A FIGHT WITH MY BOUNCER AND BROKE HIS TOOTH. HE WAS PRETTY RIPPED.

LAST TIME I SEEN DUKE, HE WAS FACE DOWN IN A SNOWBANK OUT BACK THE DEW DROP INN!

I'M GETTING CLOSER— I KNOW IT!

SIR! SIR!

AS A RECORD SNOWFALL BLANKETS COON RAPIDS...

SIR? I KNOW YOU'RE OUT HERE SOMEWHERE!

I'M SORRY I RAN OUT ON YOU, SIR! THE CAMPAIGN WAS TOO MUCH FOR ME! I THOUGHT WE'D REACHED THE END OF THE ROAD!

BUT I'VE COME TO SEE I WAS WRONG, SIR— THAT WE BELONG TOGETHER, THAT WE'VE ALWAYS BELONGED TOGETHER!

MUST...STAY... PERFECTLY... STILL.

SIR?

MY MAN'S OUT THERE SOMEWHERE —I JUST KNOW IT!

I HAVE TO FIND HIM AND MAKE THINGS RIGHT, MAKE HIM FEEL WHOLE AGAIN!

IS THAT SO WRONG? JUST WANTING TO SOOTHE HIS FEVERISH BROW, TO CHERISH HIM, TO CARE FOR HIM UNCONDITIONALLY?

THAT WAS CLOSE...

GINNY? IT'S ME...,

HEY, GIRL. HOW'D THE LAST DAY GO?

NOT WELL. SEEING ALL THOSE SMUG NEW FACES MADE ME PHYSICALLY ILL! NOT TO MENTION ANGRY!

I'M HAVING A LOT MORE TROUBLE HANDLING THIS THAN I THOUGHT I WOULD. COULD YOU COME OVER TO TALK?

SURE, HOW LONG DID RICK LAST?

ONLY A COUPLE HOURS. I DON'T KNOW WHY I'M MARRIED.

SEE, GINNY, I KNEW THIS DAY WOULD COME, BUT I'M ALARMINGLY UNPREPARED FOR IT...

I HAVE TO RE-INVENT MYSELF, AND YET I HAVEN'T A CLUE HOW TO GO ABOUT IT!

WELL, GIRLFRIEND, I'VE BEEN THERE, AND THERE'RE A FEW THINGS YOU JUST **HAVE** TO DO...

LIKE WHAT?

WELL, FIRST ORGANIZE YOUR DAY AROUND "OPRAH."

ALREADY DONE IT. GIVE ME A **LITTLE** CREDIT.

SO HOW DO YOU THINK I SHOULD MANAGE MY FORCED RETIREMENT, GINNY?

WELL, THE MOST IMPORTANT THING IS TO GIVE YOURSELF SOME TIME TO TAKE STOCK...

ALSO, GET YOUR PERSONAL LIFE IN ORDER. SINCE RICK WORKS AT HOME, YOU HAVE A WONDERFUL OPPORTUNITY TO WORK ON YOUR MARRIAGE...

THANKS FOR COMING BY, GINNY!

OH... AM I LEAVING?

IGNORE HIM. TELL ME MORE.

WHEN BLACK CONGRESSIONAL LEADERS EMERGED, THEY PAUSED TO SPEAK EXCLUSIVELY TO THIS REPORTER...

THE MEETING WAS CORDIAL. HE SEEMS NICE ENOUGH.

IN FACT, WE REALLY ONLY HAVE ONE PROBLEM WITH GEORGE W. BUSH—HE'S NOT PRESIDENT. HE DIDN'T WIN.

OTHER THAN THAT?

WELL, HE DIDN'T GIVE US NICKNAMES. EVERYONE ELSE GOT NICKNAMES.

NOT ALL BLACK LAWMAKERS WERE UNIMPRESSED. I SPOKE WITH CONSERVATIVE CONGRESSMAN CLYDE MONTANA AS HE LEFT THE WHITE HOUSE.

HE WAS GREAT! I CAN SEE WHY A ROBUST 9% OF AFRICAN-AMERICANS SUPPORT HIM! HE UNIFIES UP A STORM...

...AND HE DOES IT BY TREATING PEOPLE AS **INDIVIDUALS!**

SO YOU DIDN'T MIND BEING ASKED FOR A DRINK?

NOT AT ALL. THE LIGHTING WAS BAD.

WOW...HE'S REALLY ON BOARD, ISN'T HE?

IT'S SO EMBARRASSING.

ARI, ANY SIGNIFICANCE TO THE PRESIDENT'S FAILURE TO ASSIGN NICKNAMES TO VISITING BLACK MEMBERS OF CONGRESS?

HE CALLS THEM ALL "GUY" OR "FELLAH."

THAT'S BECAUSE THOSE NICKNAMES HAVEN'T BEEN GENERATED YET...

IT'S STILL EARLY. THE PRESIDENT HAS BEEN FOCUSING ON NICKNAMES FOR THE LEADERSHIP. RANK-AND-FILE NICKNAMES WILL COME LATER. ANY MORE QUESTIONS?

ARI!

ARI!

YES, "TOO FAT."

"HAIR BOY," YOU'RE NEXT.

ROLAND! HOW COME YOU'RE BACK ON THE TUBE?

RESTRUC-TURING...

RIGHT AFTER THE AOL-TIME-WARNER MERGER WAS APPROVED, YAP!.COM WAS FOLDED INTO CNN. 143 PEOPLE GOT THE AX!

THERE'S A HAPPY ENDING, THOUGH. I'LL NOW HAVE **BOTH** A WEB AND TV PRE-SENCE — A **LONG** WAY FROM BEING FIRED!

WHAT ABOUT THE 143 WHO WERE?

A MOVING STORY. I'LL BE COVER-ING THEIR PLIGHT.

YAP!.COM — ONCE A PROUD, CASH-FLUSH CONTENT PROVIDER...

NOW A MEMORY, JUST ONE MORE VICTIM OF THE HYPE, HUBRIS AND IRRATIONAL EXUBERANCE OF GENERATION 1.0!

WHAT WAS IT LIKE ON THE INSIDE DURING THE FINAL DAYS? FOR THE FIRST TIME, A FORMER TOP PLAYER SPEAKS OUT EXCLUSIVELY!

THE SMELL OF SMOKE IN THE COCKPIT! YOU NEVER FORGET IT...

YOU KNOW, WHEN I LOOK BACK ON YAP!.COM, I THINK OF THE EXCITE-MENT OF BEING ON THE NEW MEDIA EDGE...

...WHERE FREE CONTENT WAS POSTED EVERY HOUR, AND PEOPLE SET THEIR OWN HOURS, AND THURSDAY WAS LOBSTER NIGHT, AND THE CONCIERGE GOT NETS TICKETS FOR EVERYONE, AND...AND...

OKAY, SO THAT ONCE MADE SENSE.

THE DEMISE OF YAP!COM LEAVES THE WEB A LESS MEDIA-RICH ENVIRONMENT IN WHICH TO SURF...

AND YET THE CONTENT COMMUNITY'S TRAGIC LOSS IS THE GAIN OF THE INTERNET'S RAPACIOUS SCAVENGERS...

...WHO'VE ALREADY DESCENDED ON YAP!COM'S STILL-WARM PHYSICAL ASSETS TO GOUGE ITS DESPERATE OWNERS!

I THINK HE'S NEGO-TIATING.

OFFER LESS.

YES, IT WAS THE WORST OF TIMES...

YAP! COM — JUST LAST WEEK, A BUSTLING NEXUS OF CONTENT PRO-VISION...

TODAY, A HOLLOWED-OUT SHELL OF ITS FORMERLY INDISPENSIBLE SELF!

...ITS 143 EMPLOYEES GONE, ALONG WITH THEIR OPTIONS, THEIR PALM PILOTS, AND THEIR WITHERED DREAMS!

I'M ROLAND HEDLEY.

IT WAS THE BEST OF TIMES.

HOW MUCH FOR 143 PALM PILOTS?

OFFER 10¢ ON THE DOLLAR.

DADDY, DO YOU EVER FEEL GUIL-TY THAT WE PREY ON OTHER PEOPLE'S MIS-FORTUNES?

NO, I DON'T, SWEET-HEART...

WE'RE HELPING INVESTORS GET SOME OF THEIR MONEY BACK. AND WE'RE HELPING THE PLANET BY RECYCLING UNWANTED SUPPLIES AND FURNISH-INGS!

SO WE'RE ACTUALLY A PUBLIC SERVICE?

RIGHT. OUR BRAND SAYS WE CARE!

"myVULTURE" SAYS WE CARE?

IT SAYS WE'RE PART OF THE NATURAL ORDER.

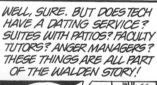

WE WANT TO PAY ATTENTION.

TAX CUTS!

WE REALLY DO.

VOUCHERS!

IT'S OUR CIVIC DUTY.

BI-PARTISANSHIP!

IF ONLY WE COULD STOP WATCHING BILL.

I DID **NOT** HAVE FINANCIAL RELATIONS WITH THAT WOMAN!

THE GREAT WAFFLER, STILL WITH US.

I DID **NOT** HAVE FINANCIAL RELATIONS WITH THAT WOMAN, MS. RICH!

THEN WHY IS THE RICH PARDON BEING INVESTIGATED BY THE FEDS?

AND WHAT ABOUT THE OTHER PARDONS TO CRONIES AND FAMILY?

WILL YOU TESTIFY BEFORE CONGRESS?

WILL RICH SEEK IMMUNITY?

WILL YOU BE RE-IMPEACHED?

THIS IS TOUGH ON THE MEDIA, ISN'T IT?

YES, SIR. REPORTERS ARE BEING CALLED OUT OF RETIREMENT.

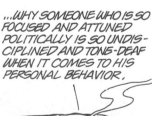

HERE COME OL' FLIP-FLOP.

I KNOW THAT A LOT OF YOU ARE WONDERING...

...WHY SOMEONE WHO IS SO FOCUSED AND ATTUNED POLITICALLY IS SO UNDISCIPLINED AND TONE-DEAF WHEN IT COMES TO HIS PERSONAL BEHAVIOR.

WELL, LET ME **TELL** YOU WHY! I...

HEY... IS THAT A DONUT SHOP OVER THERE?

THIS **WAY**, PEOPLE!

LOOK OUT! HE'S LEADING US AGAIN!

ZEKE AND J.J.'S WEBCAST WEDDING PLANS PICK UP SPEED.

OKAY, I'VE BOOKED A SERVER...

...AND ARRANGED TO STREAM THE NUPTIALS IN BOTH QUICK-TIME AND REAL VIDEO! I'VE ALSO UPLOADED THE MP3'S AND DESIGNED THE SHELL...

...LEAVING JUST ONE UNRESOLVED QUESTION...

HOW TO IN-VOLVE THE GROOM?

NO, NO, HOW TO MARKET THIS TO MY FAN BASE.

INVITATION TEMPLATE, CHECK! MP3'S, CHECK! I THINK I'VE GOT THE TECHNICAL SIDE OF OUR WEDDING JUST ABOUT COVERED...

LEAVING ME WITH NO IN-VOLVEMENT AT ALL.

OH...HEY, I'M SORRY, BABE... YOU'RE RIGHT.

TELL YOU WHAT— WHY DON'T YOU BE IN CHARGE OF SELECTING THE PRICE POINT?

...AND IT'S ATTRACTIVELY PRICED AT $29.95!

A PAY-PER-VIEW WEDDING?

CAN YOU BE-LIEVE THIS? A PAY-PER-VIEW WEBCAST?

YOUR EX IS MAD WEIRD, MIKE.

WHAT IS SHE THINKING? WHO PAYS TO SEE A WEDDING ONLINE?

NOBODY PAYS FOR ANY CONTENT ONLINE. JUST DOESN'T HAPPEN! EX-CEPT FOR PORN, OF COURSE...

NUDE BRIDES-MAIDS?

WE NEED TO ADD VALUE, MAN.

ARE YOU GOING TO COME SEE DADDY, GRAMS?

I'M AFRAID I CAN'T, HONEY. I HAVE TO CATCH A PLANE HOME.

RICK DOESN'T DO WELL ON HIS OWN. IF I'M GONE FOR TOO LONG, HE COMPLETELY FALLS APART.

WOW...

NOW **THAT** SOUNDS LIKE A GOOD MARRIAGE.

YES, I'M VERY LUCKY.

SO WAS THAT NOT THE **STUPIDEST** WEDDING YOU EVER SAW?

WELL, IT WAS DIFFERENT...

REMEMBER, YOUR MOM'S AN ARTIST. SHE VIEWS HER WHOLE LIFE AS PERFORMANCE, AS CREATIVE PROCESS...

OH, PLEASE— IT WAS GROTESQUE! RIGHT DOWN TO THE RIDICULOUS RING TATTOOS!

RING TATTOOS?

YOU GUYS SWITCHED TO THE REGIONALS, DIDN'T YOU?

UM... THERE'S A REASON PEOPLE DON'T GET MARRIED IN MARCH, HONEY.

REALLY? YOU BLEW OFF MOM'S WEDDING TO WATCH NCAA BASKETBALL?

WELL, YOU MUST ADMIT, THE WEDDING DRAGGED A BIT...

PLUS, HOW COULD I RESIST? STANFORD, DUKE, U.N.C. AND SYRACUSE ARE THE BEST FINAL FOUR* IN YEARS!

*PICKS MADE MARCH 17. IF THESE TEAMS ARE, IN FACT, THE FINAL FOUR, LOOK FOR THIS STRIP'S CREATOR TO TAKE EARLY RETIREMENT.

WISH HIM LUCK!

SIR, IN THE LAST MONTH YOU'VE KILLED RULES ON CO_2 IN THE AIR AND ARSENIC IN THE WATER, AND PROPOSED OPENING NATIONAL FORESTS TO ROADS AND DRILLING...

IS THERE ANY PART OF THE NATURAL WORLD YOU **WOULD** PROTECT?

YES, I'M COMMITTED TO PROTECTING THE NATION'S SALMONELLA SUPPLY!

SALMON-ELLA?

I BELIEVE MEN AND FISH CAN CO-EXIST PEACE-FULLY!

OKAY, SO WHY DID WE SUSPEND THE RULES CUTTING ARSENIC IN OUR DRINKING WATER?

FUZZY SCIENCE, THAT'S WHY! WE NEED GOOD, STRONG SCIENCE! GOOD SCIENCE IS WHERE OUR WINGS TAKE DREAMS!

SO UNTIL WE'VE REALLY STUDIED POLLUTED DRINKING WATER, I FAVOR A VOLUNTARY APPROACH.

TO CLEANING IT UP?

NO, NO. TO DRINKING IT.

SIR, COULD YOU EXPLAIN WHY YOU RENEGED ON YOUR CAMPAIGN PLEDGE TO LIMIT CO_2 EMISSIONS?

LOOK, CO_2 EMISSIONS IS A PART OF LIFE. IT'S CALLED EXHALING!

IN FACT, IF YOU GUYS **REALLY** WANT TO CUT CO_2 EMISSIONS, JUST STOP **TALKING** ABOUT IT!

GOOD ONE, SIR, BUT...

UH, UH, UH!

ZIP IT! ZIP IT!

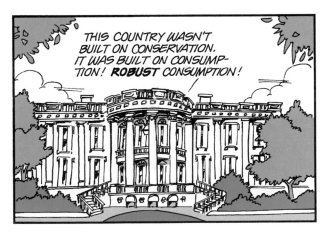

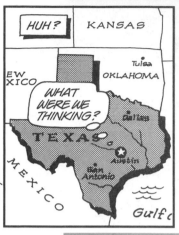

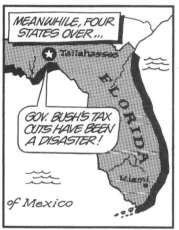

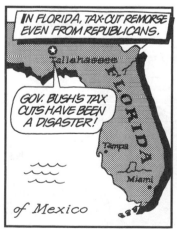